Finding New Eng
SHIPWRECKS AND T

This book is dedicated to Barry Clifford of Tisbury, Massachusetts, and to Charlie Sanderson III, of Kingston, Massachusetts. These two men may not be the best of friends, and they have, more than once, rivaled each other in locating and salvaging sunken ships and valuable treasures. Both men are dedicated and hard working researchers and hunters who have known failure and success, but have persevered amidst great adversity to complete their missions. Most important is that they were always willing to dare; this willingness places them head-and-shoulders above the many who seek fame and fortune in the world beneath the waves.

Shipwrecks are sometimes easy to find. The bow of this unknown vessel washed ashore at Sconset, Nantucket Island. Photo Courtesy of the Peabody Museum, Salem, Ma.

Cover Photos: ISBN 0-916787-05-2

New Bedford whaler WANDERER crashes ashore at Cuttyhunk Island, MA, photo courtesy of Peabody Museum, Salem, MA; scuba diver finds sunken cannon, Spanish pieces-of-eight, photos courtesy of Paul Tzimoulis; Rhode Island diver brings up British teapot from a Revolutionary War wreck, and a cannon is hauled up from the same wreck off Newport, photos courtesy of the University of Rhode Island.

INTRODUCTION

Until the early 1980's, most people looked askance at dedicated treasure hunters. They were considered a frivolous lot, forever chasing rainbows. Today, however, they emerge as sound, sensible men, many of whom have found that sunken pot of gold at the end of the rainbow. It is not treasure in the form of gold, silver and jewels that these hunters seek — and often find — but artifacts and objects of historical significance as well; items cherished by collectors and antique dealers. An old bottle or piece of china off a sunken ship can bring as much as $1,000, and a sunken cannon can be worth $10,000.

Most of the valuable items found thus far in New England waters were discovered in the shallows — sometimes in water less than twelve feet deep — easily accessible to divers geared with no more equipment than a snorkel, mask and a pair of fins.

When self-contained underwater breathing apparatus — scuba — became available in the early 1950s, many started searching for sunken ships; some scuba divers bumped into them accidentally. Various artifacts from these wrecks were hauled up and brought ashore, and some items, especially those made of wood and iron, quickly deteriorated when exposed to open air. Unfortunately, many valuable artifacts were destroyed during the early days of scuba diving, due to ignorance and poor methods of preservation. Today, however, scuba divers are learning how to preserve such items for posterity. Gold retains its brilliance no matter how long it has been immersed in water and the dream of almost every scuba diver is to find a gold bar or gold coin in the depths.

Within the last few years new devices for locating shipwrecks and treasures in the sea have been invented, or have been converted from land to underwater use. These sophisticated tools are now being used extensively by undersea archaeologists and serious treasure hunters. The side-scan sonar, for example, is an underwater device resembling a metal "fish" which is towed behind a surface craft, providing the operator on board with a line-drawing of the ocean, lake, or river floor and of any sunken ship protruding above the muddy or sandy floor. The side-scan sonar was invented by Dr. Harold Edgerton of the Massachusetts Institute of Technology, as was what the Doc calls — his "boomer and pinger". The boomer and pinger can penetrate bottom sediment, pinpointing buried metal objects and providing instantaneous top-side pictures of buried objects. Another instrument recently converted from land to sea is the magnetometer. It also has a "fish" that is towed along the surface waters behind a boat, which provides the surface operator with "anomalies" on a chart, pinpointing ferrous metals of any shape or size in the depths. That old standby — the metal detector — which has been used for many years by land treasure hunters, is now available in waterproof form. It is carried by divers who want to probe the depths for metallic items hidden under carpets of sand, silt, mud, or seaweed. All of the above have become the modern-day tools of wreck hunters — they are the reason why more shipwrecks have been located underwater in the last few years than had been found in the preceding century.

The greatest tools for hunting shipwrecks and treasures, however, remain the old book, diary, ship log, or newspaper article, hidden away in your local library or museum. Most shipwreck locations are pinpointed as a result of dilligent research. Almost every story you are about to read concerning successful finds, began in a library or museum research room. Most wreck hunters are extremely secretive about sunken ships they are researching or have recently found, but all the information at my disposal concerning valuable New England shipwrecks is presented here. For those of you who wish to hunt for a specific wreck or treasure, this book should be helpful; for you who just like to read about these adventurers and the treasures they have uncovered, I think you'll find these pages equally fascinating and stimulating.

Two-foot high ship's bell recovered in 1985, from the pirate ship WHYDAH off Cape Cod.

The Civil War battleship U.S.S. NEW HAMPSHIRE, with (inserts) Dick Peverada displaying British gold coin he found on the wreck, and Norman Russell displaying items he fashioned from the wreck's oak timbers and Paul Revere spikes. (Below) Ribs of British ship SOMERSET peek through the sand at Provincetown, Cape Cod.

I
PAUL REVERE RIDES AGAIN

Every American has heard of Paul Revere's ride and the ensuing battles at Lexington and Concord. He was one of the great heroes of that awe-inspiring time in our history, but few have heard of Paul's court-martial and disgrace after the disasterous battle at Castine, Maine. Few American history books mention the battle, yet it was the worst American naval defeat until Pearl Harbor. Even less known is the fact that in his hurried retreat from Castine, Paul, a noted arms maker and silversmith, left behind brass cannons worth $10,000 apiece today, a large trunk filled with his hand-wrought silver masterpieces, and another trunk containing his personal belongings — they remain off the coast of Maine, underwater.

The largest American naval force ever assembled in the Revolution sailed out of Boston in early July, 1779. The fleet, commanded by Captain Dudley Saltonstall, consisted of six Continental Navy ships, 13 privateers, and 20 transport barges that carried 1,300 soldiers. General Solomon Lovell and General Peleg Wadsworth commanded the troops, and Captain Paul Revere was in charge of artillery under Wadsworth. They were on their way to attack and capture the British held Fort George on the Penobscot River at Castine. The fort, situated high on a cliff, was well armed, but British General Francis McLean had only half the number of fighting men that the American generals had at their disposal. There were only three British ships anchored at the foot of the cliff, but when the American fleet arrived, Saltonstall refused to attack them. Instead, the barges came ashore, and the troops attempted to take Fort George. The battle lasted for 21 days; the British held their ground, and the Americans were forced to retreat back to the barges.

"I believe their commanders were a pack of cowards," General McLean commented a few days later, "or they would have taken me. I was in no situation to defend myself."

As the American troops reboarded the barges waiting at the river bank — under the protection of 19 American war ships — six British war ships, under the command of Sir George Collier, entered the river from the sea. Admiral Collier describes the encounter as follows: "The American ships were strung out across the mouth of the Bay in a defense line, but seeing our reinforcements, they broke formation, and the Men-of-War headed up the river, ordering their own transports to clear the way so they might continue on. When the transports, some of which were within cannon range, were left to our mercy, the rear most headed for shore . . . Seeing that the bold plan of attack had surprisingly good effect, I lost no time impressing on all sail to make a total destruction of the fleeing American ships."

The American foot soldiers were now panic stricken, either packed into transport barges drifting helplessly in the river or left on shore with neither the protection of heavy guns to support them nor vessels in which to escape. General Wadsworth ordered Paul Revere to reset his cannons up the river; however, after 21 days of taking the general's orders, Paul was fed up. He disobeyed Wadsworth's order, had his men ditch the cannons in the river, and with many of the other soldiers, began a long walk through the Maine woods back to Boston. The results of The Battle of Castine were disasterous for the Americans; over 500 soldiers and sailors killed, over 100 captured, and many wounded. The British lost 85 men. The American Navy was destroyed; six British ships defeating 39 colonial vessls.

The Beverly privateer DEFENCE, John Edmonds commanding, did not follow the other fleeing American vessels up the river, but tried to escape back out to sea. She sailed for Stockton Harbor and tried to hide from the British in a cove at Sims Island, unaware that the man-of-war HMS CAMILLA had followed her. Realizing he was out-gunned, Captain Edmonds ordered his crew to torch the 100-foot, 16 gun DEFENCE. As CAMILLA approached the cove, there was a great explosion, and the privateer brig slid beneath the surface waters, there to rest for 200 years.

Up the river, the brig SPRING BIRD, also being pursued by a British man-of-war, met the same fate as the DEFENCE. Her captain ordered her torched so she wouldn't fall into British hands. As she burned to the waterline and sank, her captain and crew swam to the nearest land. Down with the SPRING BIRD went Paul Revere's trunks of silverware and personal belongings. Paul, it seems, was as much a businessman as he was a silversmith and patriot — he had brought his hand-made silver pieces into battle with him to sell to his compatriots.

Commodore Saltonstall's flagship, WARREN, sailed to Oak Point Cove near Frankfort, Maine and was also burned to the waterline, per order of the commander. The brig ACTIVE was torched by her crew at Brigadier's Island, and the SKY ROCKET met the same fate at Fort Point Ledge. The GENERAL PUTNAM and the VENGEANCE were purposely grounded near Hampden, Maine and blown apart with explosives. The American warships HECTOR, CHARMING SALLY, BLACK PRINCE, HAZARD, DILLI-

GENCE, MONMOUTH, PROVIDENCE, and TYRANNICIDE were all scuttled in the Kenduskeag River north of Bangor, Maine, 25 miles up the Penobscot from Castine. The ships NANCY and ROVER were taken intact by the British. Over 150 American seamen lost their lives just during this naval rout by Collier's British squadron.

A few weeks later back in Boston, Commander Dudley Saltonstall was court-martialed and kicked out of the American Navy — or what was left of it. Paul Revere was court-martialed as well for disobeying General Wadsworth's order to reset the cannons up the river. "The only reason Revere walked off and didn't help us," General Wadsworth testified at the court-martial, "is because he was so damned mad that his private baggage was at stake, and was fearful that no one would pay him for it when it was lost." Although Wadsworth wanted Revere cashiered out of the Army, Paul only suffered the loss of pay and the humiliation of being reduced in rank from Captain to Lieutenant. It is ironic, however, that it was General Wadsworth's grandson who bestowed ever-lasting fame on Paul Revere. The general's grandson was poet Henry Wadsworth Longfellow.

Four of Paul Revere's discarded iron cannons were found in the murky shallows of the Penobscot River in 1953 by a construction crew working on the General Chamberlain Bridge. Another brass cannon forged in Revere's Foundry was uncovered a few years later in the river at Brewer, Maine and is valued at $10,000. It is one of only two Revere brass cannons known to exist in the world today — although there must be more of them hidden in the shallows of the Penobscot. Remnants of the vessels WARREN, GENERAL PUTNAM and VENGEANCE have also been located in the shallows by skin and scuba divers, but these charred hulks have yet to reveal anything of interest or value.

During the summer of 1972, Dean Mayhew, professor of history at Maine Academy, Castine, began a systematic search for the remains of the privateer DEFENCE. With the help of his students, he constructed a side-scan sonar to probe Stockton Harbor. After weeks of scanning the depths, the sonar chart indicated a ten-foot bump on the sea floor near Sears Island. Two of Mayhew's student divers went down to investigate. There, at a depth of 25 feet, they found the DEFENCE.

The divers reported that the DEFENCE, after enduring an explosion and 200 years in storm-tossed seas, was in remarkable condition. Mayhew went to work immediately, hauling to the surface one of her 16 six-foot swivel-mounted cannons. Both the Maine State Museum and the Institute of Nautical Archaeology offered to assist Mayhew in his underwater dig for artifacts. Archaeological experts were extremely interested in this find, for this was the first Revolutionary War privateer ever discovered in the depths, and historians knew very little about these privately owned fighting vessels. Having assembled the men, money and materials needed for a proper archaeological excavation, Mayhew and his team of experts began in earnest to salvage items from the DEFENCE in June of 1975.

Sifting through the sand into the hull of the wreck, divers first uncovered a copper caboose — or deck stove — and a large copper cooking cauldron, which were brought to the surface. Also salvaged for display at the Maine State Museum were 20 pewter spoons, some with teeth marks in them, which enabled the archeologists to determine that 17% of the crew were left handed. Many tools and navigational instruments were recovered, as well as casks and wooden meat-tags bearing the initials of the various crew members carved into them, indicating that choice cuts of meat were allotted to the officers and high ranking crew members. Pulley wheels, belaying pins, lead aprons belonging to the cannoneers, grape-shot, cannon balls, shoes, buttons, and a fancy intricately carved artillery piece, were found inside and around the wreck. Much broken glass was uncovered around the ship's white oak timbers, remnants of rum bottles and jugs that were smashed in the explosion. One earthenware jug, however, was uncovered unharmed and still in one piece.

Today, the DEFENCE remains in the sea. Although many would like to see her raised and displayed on land, "to do it," says nautical archaeologist Warren Riess, "would probably cost over a million dollars." Riess, who is assistant to David Switzer, leader of the DEFENCE excavation team, recently commented that "there is still some digging to do at the wreck site, and many more years of analysis of the items already salvaged and preserved."

Meanwhile, Maine Museum Research Director Ronald Kley is planning to lead an underwater expedition in search of the eight sunken vessels of Saltonstall's navy in the Kenduskeag River. He won't be the first to hunt for them though — a salvage crew using a diving bell went looking for them in 1819, but came up empty handed. Dean Mayhew is also still out hunting, but this time he hopes to find the brig ACTIVE off Brigadier's Island. The big find, however, would be the SPRING BIRD and Paul Revere's trunk, filled to the brim with his hand-made masterpieces.

"Just down the road apiece," as a Maine old timer might put it, is another warship with Paul Revere connections. She sits only 100 yards off the coast of Manchester, Massachusetts in 15 to 20 feet of water. Inadvertently, the Saltonstall family is involved with this shipwreck too. Former Massachusetts Senator William Saltonstall, a descendent of Commodore Dudley Saltonstall, wrote the state law pertaining to shipwrecks and sunken treasures, and in 1974 created the Massachusetts Board of Underwater Archaeology. The reason for Senator Saltonstall's interest in shipwrecks is that, in July 1923, the American Civil War Battleship U.S.S. NEW HAMPSHIRE caught fire and sank in his back yard.

It took longer to build the U.S.S. NEW HAMPSHIRE than it has taken to build any other ship in the American Navy, including aircraft carriers and nuclear submarines. Her keel was laid in 1818, the year Paul Revere died, but — because of lack of funds — it was 44 years later that she was launched, just in time for the Civil War. As in the construction of the War of 1812 battleship U.S.S. CONSTITUTION *"Old Ironsides"*, which still rides the waves at Charlestown, Massachusetts, Paul Revere's handmade copper and brass nails and spikes were used to hold together the NEW HAMPSHIRE. Both vessels were designed by noted ship-builder William Doughty. The 196-foot battleship was originally named ALABAMA; however, during the Civil War that name didn't suit the pride of the Yankee fleet, so she was renamed GRANITE STATE, and later the U.S.S. NEW HAMPSHIRE.

With a complement of 820 sailors, the NEW HAMPSHIRE trained her 74 guns on South Carolina during the war as a member of the South Atlantic blockade. After the war she served as flagship for Commodore Inman, then a supply ship and a training ship. On June 5, 1892, after a hum-drum career, she was placed out of commission and turned over to the New York Naval Militia. In July, 1923, the old wooden battleship was being towed from New York to Maine to be dismantled, but she never made her last port of call. Two of the crewmen aboard the towboat said that she was struck by lightning, another said that she just burst into flames as they cruised in heavy seas off Salem Harbor; for whatever reason, the tow-line was cut. The old battleship was free and drifting, flames licking her decks and lighting the skies. She finally nudged up to little Graves Island off Manchester and sank. She was then forgotten for another thirty years.

In the early 1950's, when skin and scuba diving became a popular sport, the U.S.S. NEW HAMPSHIRE instantly became the most popular sunken ship in New England. Her remains are in shallow water, near shore, where underwater visibility is usually good, and this made her especially attractive to weekend sports divers. Even youngsters, wearing no more equipment than mask, fins and snorkel, visit the wreck and collect authentic Paul Revere artifacts. There is hardly an underwater explorer living along the North Shore of Massachusetts who doesn't have at least one of Paul Revere's 6- to 9- inch brass spikes with "U.S." stamped into it. Although there are many more to be plucked from the wreckage of the old wooden battleship, the day is coming soon when there will be none to be found at the wreck site.

One enterprising scuba diver, Norman "Duggie" Russell of Beverly, not only has salvaged many of the NEW HAMPSHIRE's nails and spikes, but has hauled up large chunks of her oak timbers as well. Duggie fashions the wood and brass into unique wall plaques, mantlepieces, candleholders, clocks and jewelry which he sells at local shops.

Another Beverly scuba diver, Dick Peverada, made a valuable find while combing through the wreckage of the NEW HAMPSHIRE. "When I first spotted the small round object," said Peverada, "I thought it was a rock or shell, but I picked it up anyway, then realized it was gold." It was a British seven-dollar gold piece in near-mint condition, dated 1803. The coin reads, "Georgius III Dei Gratia- Britannium Rex Fedei Defensor," meaning— "George the Third, Thanks to God, King of Britain, Faithful Defender." The coin is worth over $400 today. Dick's find further increased the popularity of wreck diving on the U.S.S. NEW HAMPSHIRE.

It was all this activity, only a stone's throw from Bill Saltonstall's home, that prompted him to write the Massachusetts Underwater Archaeology Act. It allows the finder of any sunken ship that is over 100 years old, or any sunken treasure or artifact that is worth more than five thousand dollars, ownership and exclusive salvage rights to 75% of its value — the State receiving a 25% share.

When she was afloat, the U.S.S. NEW HAMPSHIRE never even came close to gaining the fame of her sister ship "Old Ironsides", but in her watery tomb, she remains the most popular sunken ship in New England's underwater fleet.

In September of 1983 the federal government informed the Massachusetts Board of Underwater Archaeology that there is one shipwreck, although she is within the three-mile area of the state's underwater territory, that remains under federal jurisdiction. The reason the federal government has stepped in to stake its claim is that the wreck is located at Cape Cod's National Seashores Park, and a local team of divers wanted to claim the wreck through the state. Today, the wreck seems to be no more than a skeleton of white oaken ribs that periodically peek through the sand at Provincetown. However, before she wrecked, she was the biggest thorn in America's side and the greatest obstacle to Paul Revere before his Midnight Ride. Henry Wadsworth Longfellow mentions the ship in his famous Paul Revere poem:

> "Just as the moon rose over the bay,
> Where swinging wide at her moorings lay,
> The 'Somerset', British man-of-war,
> A phantom ship, with each mast and spar,
> Across the moon like a prison bar,
> And a huge black hulk, that was magnified
> By its own reflection in the tide . . ."

Slowly and silently, using his wife's petticoat to muffle the oars, Paul Revere rowed around the 1,436-ton, 70-gun SOMERSET on his way from Boston to Charlestown to begin his famous ride. The SOMERSET was also the notorious man-of-war that unmercifully bombarded Charlestown and Bunker Hill during the famous battle. She paid dearly for her dastardly deeds on November 1, 1778 when she crashed into a sand bar in a storm at the tip of Cape Cod. Of the 550 British tars and marines aboard her at the time, 70 drowned and 480 were taken prisoner.

In his diary, General Joseph Otis of Barnstable mentions that the SOMERSET, using Provincetown as her home port for supplies, was trying to capture the American privateer frigate BOSTON when she sailed too close to Peaked Hill Bar near Race Point and grounded. Local blacksmith William Spenser gathered as many shopkeepers and fishermen as he could to "capture the ship and help the men in distress," but many drowned, "because it was night and the tide was coming in." There were also American prisoners aboard the wreck who were re-leased by the Provincetown and Truro townsfolk, and then they all joined in to loot the wreck. General Otis called it "riotous doings" and "wicked work", and he reported that about $150,000 in cash and merchandise was plundered from the SOMERSET.

Although 30 British officers were taken under guard to Boston by boat, the British crewmen and marines were made to walk the 125 miles to Boston, some of them freezing to death along the way. As the prisoners were marched from town to town, new details of local militia took over the responsibility of guarding them, but by the time they reached Boston on November 13th, only a few Americans were guarding them. Many of the British prisoners didn't make the jail house, either falling by the wayside from cold and exhaustion or making their escape into woods and surrounding villages. Paul Revere must have passed them on the way as he headed for the wreck from Boston, hoping he wasn't too late to get in some looting himself. He did get to the SOMERSET in time to confiscate 21 of her 70 cannons. He brought them back to Boston and set them up at Castle Island. Paul at the time was in charge of Boston Harbor defenses. What better way to fend off the British than with their own cannons. Some of these cannons remain today on the Boston Harbor islands.

Although the bulk of the SOMERSET is usually underwater and buried deep under the sand, parts of her occasionally reappear above the sand at low tide. When she emerged in 1880 and in 1886, souvenir hunters swarmed around her and walked off with various pieces of her oak frame. When she reappeared above the sand in 1976, in time for America's bicentennial, federal marshals were placed around the wreck to stop souvenir hunters from taking pieces of her. No one knows if anything of value or historical significance is hidden in or around the bleached skeleton, and unless the federal government sponsors an archaeological dig, no one will ever know. Many historians and archaeologists believe she should be excavated and the wreck properly preserved in a museum, but the eventual fate of the SOMERSET is up to Uncle Sam.

From the initial defeat of America's first naval fleet at Castine, to America's great nemesis at the tip of Cape Cod, thus is the extent of Paul Revere's ride through little known history. Because of his obsession with building ships, making cannons, procuring cannons and designing silverware, Paul Revere has left us a legacy in the sea — and many valuable bits and pieces of this legacy have yet to be found.

II
CAPE COD'S TREASURE SHIP — WHYDAH

If the SOMERSET is the most protected shipwreck in New England, the pirate ship WHYDAH, located only a few miles down the beach near the Truro-Wellfleet town line, is certainly the richest — possibly the richest in the world. At the time of her sinking in 1717, she carried an estimated $4,000,000 in gold, silver, jewels and ivory tusks, considered today to be worth possibly $400,000,000.

From the microfilm library in the Historical Department of the Boston Public Library, one can piece together this fascinating story of pirate treasure buried under only a few feet of water, 400 yards off the beach at Wellfleet, Cape Cod. There is the Boston Court transcript of the nine surviving pirates, with a detailed report on the subsequent execution of six of them. There is the journal of Captain Cyprian Southback — the man sent to Cape Cod by the Governor of Massachusetts to confiscate the treasure, and there is a small book written by Cotton Mather, the leading Boston minister of that Puritanical period, titled: *A Brief Relation of Remarkables in the Shipwreck of Above One Hundred Pirates, Who Were Cast Away in the Ship WHIDO, on the Coast of New England, April 26, 1717*. From this material, the true tragedy of avarice and high adventure unfolds, rivaling Robert Louis Stevenson's *Treasure Island* and providing enough documental evidence to "shiver the timbers" of any modern day treasure hunter.

Samuel Bellamy was a merchant seaman from the west of England. As a young man he traveled from Europe to ports in Maine, Rhode Island and Massachusetts. He was tall, he was dark, and he was handsome. He was also a drinker and a womanizer, but then again, so were many seamen in those swashbuckling days of the early 18th century. His idol since boyhood was Captain Avery, also from the west of England, known throughout the world as "King of the Pirates." Avery had organized a band of over 1,000 cut-throats that raided vessels off India and Africa from their pirate haven stronghold on the island of Madagascar. He was England's Robin Hood of the Seven Seas, occasionally giving money to the poor and often stealing from the very rich. His letters home, dripping with intrigue and adventure, were published in England at about the turn of the century, when Sam Bellamy was but a boy.

Sam didn't set out to be a pirate, but he was excited about one of Avery's accounts which mentioned a richly laden Spanish galleon wrecked on a shallow water reef in the Bahamas. He discussed searching for this treasure galleon with his pal Paul Williams of Nantucket, and they decided to drift down the East Coast to warmer climates in search of Spanish gold and silver. They made their plans for the trip at Higgins Tavern in Eastham on the Cape where Sam met 15 year old Maria Hallett and seduced her. Whether Sam knew that he had gotten Maria pregnant is not recorded, but if he did know, it probably hastened his plans to head for the Caribbean.

Sam and Paul searched diligently for Avery's Spanish galleon but found nothing. Without a shilling to their names, destitute in a strange, hot, brutal land, they decided to do what most other down-and-outers were doing in the West Indies — pirating. They joined a small group of fortune seekers led by Louis Lebous, who sailed from the Lesser Antilles, attacking small merchant ships and fishing boats. This proved to be fairly successful, however Sam sought bigger and better things in life. Taking a larger than usual merchantman prize — the sloop POSTIL-LION — Bellamy insisted he command her; Lebous and the other pirates agreed. Sam Bellamy was now a pirate-chief. He grew a long black beard that hung to his chest, and his silky black hair flowed over his shoulders and down his back — his men called him "Black Bellamy".

In the autumn and winter of 1716-17 Bellamy and his pirates took many more, richer prizes, among them the sloop MARY ANNE which he turned over to Paul Williams, the treasure galleon SENORA DELA-CONCEPTION, the British ship SAINT MICHAEL and the galley SULTANA, which he decided to use as the flagship of his fleet. He then turned the POSTILLION over to Lebous to command. On February 20 Bellamy's marauders were sailing in three vessels off Point O'Pines, Cuba when they spied a sleek English galley, heading for Europe. Because of her size and the 23 cannons on her deck, Bellamy was reluctant to attack her immediately. He signaled his sloop commanders to fly English ensigns from their topmasts and not the Jolly Roger, hoping to fool the galley commander into thinking that they were also British merchantmen. The three pirate ships followed the galley at a safe distance for three days until they closed in on the third night under the protection of darkness. Captain Lawrence Prince, commander of the slave galley WHYDAH, realized too late that he was being surrounded by pirate vessels. He fired off two of his cannons, hoping to frighten them away, but Bellamy's boarding parties were ready to do their bloody work. Captain Prince, to Bellamy's surprise, surrendered his vessel without a fight.

Prior to being captured, the WHYDAH had sailed from England to Guinea, Africa where she took on hundreds of black slaves, then dropped them off at Jamaica. She was heading back home with a cargo of indigo, gold dust and elephant tusks when Bellamy caught up with her. Sam was so pleased with this seaworthy vessel and her timid captain that he transferred Captain Prince and his crew to the SULTANA, allowing them to continue on to England, and he took command of the WHYDAH. He first, of course, placed all the gold, silver and jewels he had collected over the previous months in the hold where the slaves had been kept. In addition to 200,000 pounds of silver, mostly Spanish pieces-of-eight, were a lesser quantity of gold doubloons and gold "dust", all stashed below decks in 180 leather bags, each weighing about 50 pounds. Also included were "enough precious jewels to ransom a Princess," as revealed by Tom Davis at the pirate court trial in Boston many months later. It was further reported at the trial that seven of the SULTANA's cannons were transferred to the WHYDAH.

Now, with a crew of 142, some of them forced men from crews of other vessels he had pirated, Bellamy sailed the WHYDAH up the East coast of America. Paul Williams followed in his sloop with some 20 men, but Lebous and his pirate crew decided to stay behind. Of Virginia and the Carolinas, Bellamy and his pirates overtook three British vessels and confiscated their cargoes of rum and various food stuffs. Off Rhode Island they captured another merchant vessel under the command of Captain Beers of Newport. They packed his cargo aboard the WHYDAH, sank Beers' sloop and set him adrift in a rowboat — he reached Block Island safely a day later.

About 60 miles off Nantucket Island the pirates encountered another little merchant vessel heading for New York, the snow MARY ANN from Dublin — not to be confused with the sloop MARY ANNE commanded by Williams, that had fallen a day in sailing time behind the WHYDAH coming up the coast. The Dublin MARY ANN was carrying a cargo of Madeira wine, an unexpected prize which may have been the downfall of Black Bellamy and his pirate crew. Along with several casks of wine, Bellamy took her commander, Captain Andrew Crumpstey and seven of her ten man crew aboard the WHYDAH. Then he placed seven of his pirates aboard the MARY ANN with Tom Baker in charge.

A Northeast storm had been threatening for days; now whitecaps were kicking up the surface waters, and darkness was setting in. So pirate Baker, a Rhode Islander who knew these waters better than most, rigged a lantern to the mast of the MARY ANN. Bellamy agreed to follow the MARY ANN through the storm to a protected harbor on the seaward side of the Cape. As they sailed in, the storm increased its fury.

High rolling swells, stinging salt spray and Madeira wine blinded the WHYDAH crew, causing them to lose sight of the MARY ANN that sailed miles ahead of them. Then came the awesome boom of crashing breakers. The 300-ton galley, overburdened with cannons, crewmen and contraband, scraped bottom and slid across an underwater sand bar. Bellamy fought desperately to control her, as wind and wave forced her into the sand cliffs at Wellfleet. Although he managed to turn her back out to sea, in the process the keel was twisted and crushed into the bottom sand. In the midst of howling winds, booming breakers and screaming men, the WHYDAH quivered helplessly, rolled and turned bottom up, spewing her cargo, cannons and crew into he raging surf. Her teak deck fell out and drifted for a while with men clinging to it. Her hull split apart, its valuable contents sinking into the depths. Of the 100 pirates who were flung ashore in the giant breakers, only two managed to claw their way up the high sand cliff to safety — John Julian, a Cape Cod Indian and Tom Davis, a Welch carpenter. Both had been forced into piracy in the West Indies by Black Bellamy, the would-be "King of the Pirates", who went down to the bottom of the sea with his ship.

Meanwhile the MARY ANN crew were having their own problems about eight miles down the beach. The MARY ANN hit a sand bar too and slid onto Pocket Island off the coast of Orleans. High and not so dry, sitting in the leaking hold of the MARY ANN, the seven pirates and three Irish crewmen — Thomas Fitzgerald, Alex Mackonachie and John Dunavan — prayed fervently for deliverance as they drank wine. Their prayers were answered at dawn when two Eastham fishermen rowed out to Pocket Island and transported them, along with a barrel of wine, safely to the mainland. The ten survivors walked to the home of John Cole, where they sat around the fireplace all morning drinking more wine. When John Cole realized that some of his guests were pirates, he sent his six year old son to fetch the sheriff. When Sheriff Joseph Doane arrived at Cole's house, the seven pirates ran out the back door, and, for no apparent reason, the three Irish crewmen ran off with them. The ten shipwreck victims then came to Eastham's Crosby Tavern where they intended to steal horses. Instead, tempted by the aroma of the taproom, they lingered so long that the sheriff and his posse caught up with them. There, the pirates and crewmen were arrested and carted off to Boston. It was then that they were told of the ill fated WHYDAH and the survival of only two of her crew.

Julian and Davis had stumbled two miles through the storm to the home of Wellfleet fisherman Samuel Harding. At daylight, Tom Davis accompanied Sam Harding to the wreck site. Some treasure, mostly pieces-of-eight, had washed ashore. Splintered wood and timbers covered the beach for miles as did many battered bodies, some naked. Before noon there were hundreds of Cape Codders picking through the debris on the beach and pocketing silver coins. The surf was still pounding the beach. There was no way to get to the wreck itself, although a portion of it was within sight some 700 yards offshore.

A Colonel Buffet of Cape Cod wrote to Massachusetts Governor Samuel Shute on April 29, 1717, three days after the shipwreck, stating that, "a sloop was at anchor near the shipwreck, but next morning sailed off with 18 men onboard her and a small boat that they had taken on the craft with four men." This was probably pirate Paul Williams and his crew, arriving a day after the storm. One wonders, however, if the four men in the boat were part of his MARY ANNE crew or four additional survivors from the WHYDAH. On May 25 the Governor sent an armed sloop out of Boston in pursuit of Williams. Next day, he and his crew in the MARY ANNE were seen heading south in Vineyard Sound — and haven't been seen since.

When Governor Shute was informed that Cape Codders were literally picking up a small fortune at the "Table-Land" beaches in Wellfleet, he sent his friend Captain Cyprian Southback to the Cape to confiscate the treasure for the Commonwealth. Southback arrived at Wellfleet six days after the disaster. On that day he wrote a letter to the Governor stating, "the people here are very strife, and will not give up one thing of what they got on the wreck." He called Samuel Harding "as guilty as the pirates." Southback and his small police force searched almost every house and barn within twenty miles of the wreck site and did recover some of the pirate booty, hidden in local cellars and attics. Because of bad weather that continued to kick up the surface waters off the seaward side of the Cape, Southback wasn't able to get a boat through the surf to visit the wreck site until May 10. Even then, he could only peer into the murky, stirred up water to guess how much treasure remained in the shallows — it was already buried under bottom sand. He then packed into his small sloop what little treasure he had collected from the reluctant Cape Codders and headed back to Boston. As he rounded Provincetown into Cape Cod Bay, he was overtaken by another sloop and pirated of the loot he had recovered. To this day, no one knows if this was the work of Paul Williams or of the Eastham and Wellfleet villagers who just wanted to get their beach collections back.

The surviving pirates languished in Boston jail for almost six months before their trial in October. During that time the three Irish MARY ANN crewmembers were set free, and pirate Thomas South died of consumption. John Julian the Indian, although found innocent, was sold into slavery; Tom Davis, also considered a forced man, was freed, and he returned to Wales. On the chilly morning of November 15, 1717 the other six were accompanied by Reverend Cotton Mather and twenty armed guards to a long strip of land in Boston Harbor facing Charlestown. "Pirates Baker and Hoof appeared very distinguished and penitent," wrote Mather, "but John Brown broke into furious expressions, which had in them too much of the language he had been used to." Vanvorst sang a Dutch hymn; Quinter tried to sing, but when he opened his mouth nothing came out. John Shaun, the Frenchman, kept his mouth shut. Cotton Mather addressed the crowd of Bostonians who had come to witness the spectacle. "They were rich people, 'tis true," he said, "but then, what riches they had, they did not come by honestly." As the words rolled off his lips, the eyes of the six pirates stared blankly out to sea, their bodies swaying to and fro in the icy wind.

Local legend holds the reason Black Sam Bellamy was sailing off Cape Cod was that he was returning to his sweetheart Maria Hallet with his treasure, so that they could live happily ever after. More than likely he was heading for the Maine wilderness where he could set up a pirate haven, as did his hero Captain Avery in Madagascar. Maria, however, during Sam's long absence, was anything but happy. While he was away, she bore his illegitimate child, was banished from Eastham and — while hiding out in a barn — lost her baby when it choked to death on a piece of straw.

It was 146 years after Sam Bellamy and his 140 pirates drowned off Wellfleet, that famous American naturalist Henry David Thoreau decided to search for the WHYDAH's sunken treasure. He was told by Cape Cod oysterman John Newcomb that the galley's iron caboose — a large metal stove used to cook meals for the slaves — could be seen at low tide protruding from the sand a few hundred yards offshore. Thoreau and his friend William DeCosta spent weeks at the site in the summer of 1863 and recovered some 20 pieces-of-eight from the shallows. Since then, usually after a Nor'east storm, many beachcombers continue to visit the outer Cape shore, climbing down the 100-foot cliffs to sift through the wet sand of Marconi Beach in search of silver tidbits tossed in by the thunderous breakers. The famous Italian physicist and Nobel Prize winner Guglielmo Marconi sent the first wireless telegraph radio message across the Atlantic to Europe on the Highland sand cliff overlooking this beach.

On November 7, 1982 Cape Cod's treasure ship WHYDAH was officially "arrested" by United States federal marshals. A Martha's

Vineyard scuba diver named Barry Clifford, who had been searching for the WHYDAH for some ten years, found a clay pipe stem, a hand-made nail and two pieces of 18th century pottery in 15 feet of water some 200 yards off Marconi Beach. Appearing before the Massachusetts Board of Underwater Archeology on February 25, 1983, Clifford was granted a permit to work on the wreck site within a 2000 yard radius of his find.

Clifford anchored the 70-foot work boat VAST EXPLORER II — originally built for the U.S. Navy — over the wreck site. Attached to her stern are two huge aluminum cylinders called mailboxes which, when lowered, divert the power of the ship's twin 240 horsepower diesel engines directly downward, easily blowing away bottom sand and creating 15 foot craters underwater within minutes. Throughout 1983, the mailboxes uncovered only a few iron fittings and a twisted rudder strap. Clifford was not disappointed; in the shallows only a few hundred yards from where the boat was anchored, William Newman found 12 Peruvian minted silver coins, pieces-of-eight, all dated pre-1717 — one piece dated 1663.

One setback for Clifford, however, was that the Board granted one-square mile permits to two other salvage companies to work North and South of Clifford's claim. There is presently a 400 yard buffer area between the three treasure hunting sites. To the South, off Nauset Light Beach, is the Old Blue Fishing Company. They have thus far found pottery, ship's nails, musket shot and a cannon ball. To the North of Clifford, working off Cahoon Hollow Beach, is the Provincetown Ocean Marine Diving Company. Their search has thus far uncovered one piece-of-eight, a button, oak rib, gudgeon, breast hook and a gold coin dated 1713.

On the last day of July, 1984, diver Rob Mclung, after investigating one of the blow-holes created by the VAST EXPLORER's mailboxes, exploded to the surface, cheering. "We've found her," he shouted to Barry Clifford who was on deck, "there are cannons and coins everywhere down there." "Well," said Barry matter-of-factly, with a wry grin, "I guess we've got ourselves a pirate ship!" For the remaining twelve weeks, before Cape Cod's notorious rough seas made diving impossible, Clifford's diving crew recovered 3,300 silver coins. Most were Spanish pieces-of-eight, dated 1638 to 1715, all in near perfect condition. A few were coins from England, France and the Netherlands. One half-dollar sized Spanish coin, dated 1653, is so rare that it is valued at $40,000. Spanish gold doubloons, looking like they were minted yesterday, were also recovered, and chunks of gold bars and gold chains, cut into pieces supposedly to make equal shares for all the pirates. The smaller chunks of gold had little holes bored into them, possibly strung on a cord to make valuable pirate necklaces. The most remarkable discovery, however, was that the blow-hole was carpeted with gold dust, tiny gold nuggets that the divers scooped into plastic bags and hauled to the surface. They also uncovered gold rings and a two-inch gold snuff spoon.

Of the twenty-seven British and Spanish cannons they found, three were salvaged, but so far, there have been few pirate artifacts. One of the first artifacts to be brought up was an encrusted broad-sword with a hole cut into its balde, where a pirate apparently fitted a gold coin. A flintlock musket was recovered, which is being restored, and has its 18th century manufacturer's mark embedded into it. Silver buttons, brass and pewter clothing clasps, a set of interlocking pewter weights, a gold mariner's sundial, and a pewter mortar jar with the letter "W" scratched into it, capped off the 1984 treasure hunting season for Barry Clifford.

Even with all this treasure found, many Massachusetts archaelogists were not convinced that Clifford had found the WHYDAH, and thought he might be finding valuables from some other sunken ship. Because of red-tape concerning Clifford's rights to disturb the sandy bottom off Wellfleet, his precious diving season was cut short in 1985. In August, however, the VAST EXPLORER was again over the treasure-trove site, where thousands more coins, and bags full of gold-dust were brought to the surface. The value of the treasure thusfar recovered, is estimated at over $6,000,000, and as Barry Clifford says, "we've just scratched the surface."

Probably the most important find to Barry came in October, 1985, just before the divers were ready to haul anchor for the winter. A brass ship's bell, heavily encrusted, measuring two-feet high and two-feet in diameter, was uncovered in the sandy bottom of a blow-hole. It took almost a day to scrape the bell clean, but the result was worth the wait. Inscribed on the bell was: "The WHYDAH Galley-1716". No one could doubt Barry Clifford now. It took him exactly three years to forever close the mouths of the many doubting Thomases.

"My duty now," says Clifford, "is to protect and preserve the remains of the WHYDAH, and to hopefully display all we've found and have yet to find, to the public in a museum. After all," he concludes with pride, "it's the only pirate ship that has ever been found underwater," and it's certainly the richest prize ever uncovered in the depths off New England — and possibly, the world. Only time and a lot of diving and digging off Wellfleet will tell.

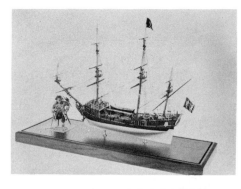

Model of British galley identical to Pirate Bellamy's vessel WHYDAH. (Right) State Geologist Joseph Sinnott, Director of the Underwater Archaeological Commission, stands with bust of Marconi, overlooking Marconi Beach and WHYDAH excavation site. (Below) Is VAST EXPLORER II and her salvage crew off Wellfleet, including, (left to right) expedition leader Barry Clifford, New York Judge John Levin, and John F. Kennedy, Jr., son of former U.S. President.

Photos by Maritime Explorations, Inc. Ship Model courtesy of The American-Marine Model Gallery, Salem, and Nightowl Productions, Nahant, MA.

III
CURSE OF THE GENERAL ARNOLD

It was Christmas 1775, and it was snowing hard. General George Washington had ordered him to lead a 700 man army made up of New Englanders through the wilderness to capture Quebec. In the blinding blizzard he attacked the fortified city, but the attack failed, and he was severely wounded. For his efforts the daring and ambitious General Arnold was promoted to Brigadier General by the Continental Congress, but this discontented hero was already contemplating treason. Months later he contacted the British to warn them of another proposed attack by the Americans on Canada. In May of 1779, upon the capture of British spy John Andre, it was discovered that General Benedict Arnold was a traitor. However, he managed to escape capture and joined the British army. He later led a British invasion on his hometown of New London, Connecticut and prompted the massacre of American troops at Fort Griswold.

It was Christmas 1778, and it was snowing hard. The 100-foot brigantine GENERAL ARNOLD — named for the gallant hero of Quebec — was at anchor off Nantasket Road, Boston Harbor. At 6:00 a.m. she weighed anchor and, in company with the privateer REVENGE, set sail for the Carolinas. The ARNOLD carried twenty guns, a detachment of marines and a cargo of military supplies for the American troops who were attempting to stop the British from cutting off the South from the Northern colonies. Her commander was Captain James Magee, an Irish born American patriot, who was looking forward to meeting up with the British, his life long enemy. Before the day was over, however, he would lose his ship to a greater enemy, the enraged sea. Of the 105 men and boys who sailed with him, 81 would die a horrible death, and the others — all but himself — would be crippled for life.

As the privateers sliced across Massachusetts Bay under full sail heading for the open sea, the wind picked up, quickly turning into a Nor'east blizzard. Captain Barrows of the REVENGE decided to ride out the storm off Cape Cod. Magee felt that his ship could better weather the storm in Plymouth Harbor behind the protective headland of Gurnet Point. But the ARNOLD's anchor wouldn't hold, and she began to drift into the long harbor.

Magee had his men dismount 16 of the deck cannons and store them below to add weight to the hull and give the vessel stability. Her sails were furled and the topmast struck, but nothing seemed to stop the ARNOLD's dragging anchor. The storm intensified, spewing waves over the bow that quickly turned to ice. The vessel yanked at the anchor cable like a bucking bronco — then the cable parted. The ARNOLD sailed backwards into the harbor, bumped over a sand bar and scraped to a sudden stop, landing atop a shallow water sand flat. She was only a mile from shore, not far from America's most famous rock where the Pilgrims had landed 158 years before.

At first Magee and his men thought they could lighten the vessel and slide her over the flat to shore. With axes they cut down her masts, but the weighted hull was already sinking into the sand, cracking her boards and leaking salt water into her hold. Icy waves washed over the main deck, and, as the captain later reported, "the quarter-deck was the only place that could afford the most distant prospect of safety." Magee goes on to say that, "within a few hours presented a scene that would shock the least delicate humanity. Some of my people were stifled to death with the snow; others perished with the extremity of the cold, and a few were washed off the deck and drowned."

There were a few bottles and casks of brandy and wine in the cargo, and many crew members ventured below into the half flooded hold to drown themselves in liquid warmth. Some were drunk before Captain Magee realized that they had broken into the stores. He pleaded with them to pour the brandy into their shoes or boots to prevent frostbite of their toes rather than pouring it down their gullets. Some obeyed, but those who didn't were dead by next morning. Those huddled together on the quarter-deck, their clothes first drenched then frozen to their bodies, covered themselves with the brigantine's sails in an effort to escape the salt spray and snow. By the morning of the 26th, thirty of them were frozen to death. The blizzard continued. Although they could see but a shadow of land through the falling snow, Magee fired his signal gun in hopes of alerting the townfolk of their dilemma. Three crewmen managed to launch the privateer's longboat into the wild sea, then started rowing to shore, but they were lost sight of and never heard from again.

Late in the afternoon when there was a short break in the storm, the people of Plymouth sent dories out from shore, however none of them could make it to the stranded vessel. Choppy seas, ice-flows and contrary wind and currents deemed their rescue mission impossible. They decided that the only way to the ARNOLD was to build a causeway of ice and snow one mile long out to the sand flat. Working throughout the night and well into the next day and night, the people of Plymouth accomplished what seemed impossible — they built a road out to the distressed privateer.

Meanwhile the shipwreck victims spent a second and third night on the quarter-deck in sub-freezing temperatures. The living feared going to sleep, knowing that if they did, they probably would not wake up again. In an attempt to block out wind and waves, they piled the dead bodies of their comrades around them. The ARNOLD sank deeper into the sand, knee deep water now covering the main deck. In an effort to keep his remaining crewmen and marines alive, Captain Magee requested — then demanded — that the men keep walking around and exercising on the little deck in order to maintain their circulation. He was especially anxious about two boys aboard: Connie Marchant, age 10 and Barny Downs, age 15. Magee prodded them to walk in place even though they were both so exhausted and frozen they could hardly stand. He urged them over and over again not to give up. Marchant later said, "I ascribe my preservation mainly to the reiterated efforts of Captain Magee."

On Monday morning, December 28th when the ice causeway was completed, the people of Plymouth passed over the ice to the wreck. "It was a scene unutterably awful and distressing," writes Plymouth's Doctor Thatcher. "The ship was sunk ten feet in the sand; the waves had been for about thirty-six hours sweeping the main deck, and even here they were obliged to pile together dead bodies to make room for the living. Seventy dead bodies, frozen into all imaginable postures, were strewn over the deck, or attached to shrouds and spars; about thirty exhibited signs of life, but were unconscious whether in life or death. The bodies remained in the posture in which they died, the features dreadfully distorted. Some were erect, some bending forward, some sitting with the head resting on the knees, and some with both arms extended, clinging to spars or some parts of the vessel."

Sleds and slabs of wood were used to carry the survivors and the stiffened corpses over the ice road to shore. The dead were piled in the Plymouth Courthouse, the living brought to local homes to spend agonizing hours thawing out. Nine of the living joined the dead within a week. At the wreck site, the Plymouth rescuers had a difficult time determining who was dead and who was alive, for most of the survivors could not move a muscle. Young Barnabas Downs could not move or utter a sound but could see that some of the frozen dead were being dropped in the water and pulled by ropes over to the ice road and awaiting sleds. As he was being picked up with the rope tied around him, thought to be dead, he blinked his eyes rapidly, in hopes that his rescuers would see that he was still alive. One rescuer noticed, and the Barnstable boy was saved. It took two days of agonizing pain for his body to thaw, and a few days later both his feet had to be amputated. Although he did live 40 more years, he spent the rest of his life walking on his knees. Little Cornelius Marchant of Martha's Vineyard lived to be 70 years old, but he too was crippled for life.

When the local minister, Chandler Robbins, came to the courthouse to perform funeral services for the 81 dead men, the horror that greeted him caused him to faint on the courtroom floor. An attempt was made to unfreeze some of the bodies so they would fit into the coffins, but most remained in their grotesque postures. A mass grave was dug at Plymouth's Burial Hill where 66 ARNOLD crewmen and marines were buried together. Some of the bodies were frozen to each other in a death grip and could not be separated. Captain John Russell, commander of the marines and David Hill, his first lieutenant, hugged each other in death. Since there was no way to break their grip, they were buried together in one grave.

Captain James Magee didn't even suffer frostbite; however, constant anguish over the loss of his ship and men brought him to an early grave in 1801 at age 51. His one regret was his decision to turn into Plymouth Harbor to escape the brunt of the storm, since his counterpart, Captain Barrows of the REVENGE, had successfully ridden out the storm off Cape Cod.

Magee skippered merchant ships out of Salem, Massachusetts for the remainder of his life, including the famous ASTREA that opened American trade with China. Whenever in home port at Christmas, Magee called for a reunion of the 24 ARNOLD survivors, assisting any who were destitute with a gift from his own wages. At his request, when he died he was buried with the ARNOLD crew at Burial Hill, Plymouth.

It was Christmas 1976, and it was snowing hard, but I was finding it hard to get into the Christmas spirit. As Director of the Massachusetts Board of Underwater Archaeological Resources, I was being sued by an insistent, aggressive fellow named Charles Sanderson III, the Director of Plymouth's International Military Museum. I had never been sued before, and I didn't like it. Also, like Irish Captain Magee, I had hereditary distrust for anyone who had a number following his name.

Charles Sanderson III claimed he had found the remains of the GENERAL ARNOLD in Plymouth Harbor. He said that he had pinpointed the location of the wreck through an old diary he had found in the attic of his home in Kingston. The diary was kept by one of Sanderson's ancestors who had helped build the ice road in 1778 and had taken ARNOLD survivors into his Kingston home. In March of 1976 a 75-foot section of a sunken ship appeared above the sand at low tide on White Flat in Plymouth Harbor. Sanderson said it was the ARNOLD, and he filed claim for ownership of the wreck through the state Board, as did four other individuals and organizations on or about the same time. The five claimants appeared before the eight member Board of Underwater Archaeology at a seven hour hearing in Boston on September the 9th, each insisting that he was the first to discover the wreck. It was a difficult hearing to sit through and even more difficult to decide who was entitled to claim the wreck.

The prestigious Pilgrim Society of Plymouth was first to acknowledge discovery of the wreck at White Flat on April 2, 1976. Lawrence Geller, a director of the Society, stated that although the general location of the ARNOLD had been known for years, she had been buried under some six feet of sand and had begun to surface only recently. It was thought that the building of the Plymouth breakwater — now protecting the inner harbor — had altered currents and wave action, pulling the top layers of sand off White Flat and exposing a ten foot portion of the wreck which had been buried for almost 200 years. Scuba diver Barry Clifford — of WHYDAH fame — came before the Board to insist that on April 1 he was first to sight the wreck protruding above the sand-flat. Local fisherman Stephen Loziak said that he first noticed the exposed timbers at low tide, and that he took Clifford out in his boat to investigate the wreck on March 30 — Clifford disagreed. David Bowley of Kingston reported that, after searching for the wreck for days on the expansive sand-flat, he hired a plane and, flying low over the harbor, was first to spot the wreck from the air. Sanderson, meanwhile, had rowed out to the wreck site, tied a bouy to the timbers and removed an eight-sided wooden peg, called a treenail, from one of the timbers. Treenails, which were used by shipwrights on vessels prior to 1780, identified this wreck as having been built prior to or during the American Revolution, but, of course, did not identify her as the GENERAL ARNOLD. Since the Pilgrim Society was the first to request in writing to the Board, they were granted a title-permit to excavate the wreck. Charles Sanderson disagreed with the Board's decision, mainly because the Pilgrim Society had not included compass bearings of the wreck location in their permit request. He sued the Board. Just before Christmas, I, as its Director, had to appear before the State Attorney General to justify our decision.

While I was awaiting a verdict by the Attorney General, a strange and surprising turn of events transpired which remains a mystery to me to this very day. The Pilgrim Society, in a letter to the Board, withdrew their claim to the wreck at White Flat. "We do not believe this wreck is that of the GENERAL ARNOLD," the letter read, "and further research into the subject reveals that the ARNOLD was repaired and later sailed for Europe." Indication was that the wreck at White Flat was nothing more than an old coal barge. Sanderson was next in line to claim the wreck. "The salvaging of the ARNOLD is not an established fact," Sanderson told news reporters. "There is no proof that the wreck in question is not the ARNOLD." Sanderson happily accepted the hand-me-down claim to the White Flat wreck from the Board, and I was relieved that the dispute had been resolved. If Sanderson wanted to salvage a Colonial coal barge, that was his business.

A few weeks later, a Boston television station produced a three-part expose documentary on the evening news, revealing that the GENERAL ARNOLD was not only repaired, refloated and returned to duty during the Revolution, but was later captured by the British and renamed the AMSTERDAM. She was retained as a British merchantman sailing out of Halifax until 1830. The report depicted museum director Charles Sanderson III as trying to deceive the public that his coal barge was a famous Revolutionary War privateer.

When Sanderson uncovered a piece of coal at the wreck site, I was convinced that the Pilgrim Society was right in forfeiting their claim. Even though the Pilgrim Society had located a document detailing the salvage of the ARNOLD, I did wonder why the Colonials would exert so much effort to remove a crushed hull from the soggy quicksand. I could understand their attempting to salvage the cargo, but why the ship? Also, once it was known throughout America that Benedict Arnold had defected to the enemy some five months after the shipwreck, I would think the vessel would become a scourge to the superstitious Yankees, not worthy of flying the American flag again. Even the shipwreck survivors, including Captain Magee, never mentioned the ARNOLD by name, once it was known that the General was a traitor. They called her "the ship" or "the brig", and in their writings years later did not call her by name. Many of the survivors, including Cornelius Marchant and Barnabas Downs, believed that the ship was cursed from the moment Benedict Arnold decided to join the British. Many historians believe now, as did the ARNOLD crew then, that the moment of defection was on Christmas Eve 1778, when the General attended a party at the home of a Philadelphia Tory.

It was July 4, 1982, and it was hot as hell. I got a phone call from Charles Sanderson III. "Come to Plymouth as soon as you can," he said. "I've found the main part of the wreck, and I want to show you the items I'm bringing up." He had found a large section of the wreck, some 200 yards from the exposed timbers that everyone had been fighting over earlier. "Believe me, she's not a coal barge... Her deck is still intact, and some of the wreck shows out of water at dead low tide." Although somewhat skeptical, I was standing in Sanderson's boat within two hours, about a mile off the Plymouth coast, watching his three scuba divers bring up burlap bags filled with sand and silt that they dropped at our feet.

The tide was high, and a swift current flowed over the wreck site. Some 15 feet below the divers scooped bottom silt into their bags, while on deck, Sanderson on his hands and knees gingerly clawed through the soggy debris the divers dumped before us. He began picking out pieces of glass and broken ceramic, studying each little piece, like a mad scientist searching for a missing link. He uncovered a broken clay pipe bowl with the stem intact. A star was hand carved into the bowl. His eyes twinkled with triumph as he handed it to me to inspect. "I have the rest of this at home," he smiled. "I found it yesterday... And this large piece of ceramic with the oak tree painted on it," he said, holding up the jagged ceramic object covered with algae and weed. "This is the missing piece I've been searching for to finish the bowl I've been mending together. It's American, mid 18th century, and there's no doubt about it." Then came the top of an old wine jug with the stopper still in it, two halves of the handle of a tortoise-shell knife, three balaying pins, a bag full of cannon shot.

The divers were up with three more filled burlap bags. They dumped them on deck and disappeared over the side as I got on my hands and knees to help Charlie sift through it all. I was excited, for this was a real treasure hunt. We uncovered a wooden scabbard, a galley knife, a granite cannonball, more pieces of pottery, and three leather shoes, looking like they had just come from Thom McAn. "We've found a lot of these shoes," said Sanderson. "Maybe that was part of the shipment going to the troops down South." I was in awe. "Yesterday my son Chuck found a mess kit while walking around the wreck at low tide," he said matter-of-factly. "The mess kit was a wooden bucket that Colonial sailors used to keep their personal belongings in — it's in near perfect condition, and the only other one like it was found on the sunken privateer DEFENCE at Castine, Maine." Sanderson could tell by the dumbfounded look on my face that he had a convert — this certainly wasn't a coal barge. "Oh, by the way," he added, sealing the lid on any possible skepticism I might have, "a set of initials were scratched into the bottom of the mess kit, 'J.C.', probably stand for Josiah Crockett, who was one of the ARNOLD's crewmen... We also found a wooden scabbard two days ago that had initials carved in it too — 'W.D.' — maybe belonging to William Dunham, one of the ARNOLD's marines."

Without yet removing the well preserved deck on the wreck, Sanderson's divers have so far brought up many iron cannonballs, pottery, another clay smoking pipe, cuttlery, an eating dish still in one piece, ballast stones, rum bottles and two whole chicken eggs, without one crack in their blackened shells. These items were all found lying around the wreck by divers Jay Barrett, Steve Rowell and Chuck Sanderson — excuse me, Charles Sanderson IV.

Nautical archaeologist Warren Reiss, with a team of five other archaeologists, spent one week in late September 1983 at the GENERAL ARNOLD wreck site measuring her stem, stern and frame ends plus her hull outline at low tide. Some two feet of her hull is now visible above the sand. They then inspected her 75 foot port section, some 200 yards away from the main wreck near Plymouth Harbor's main channel. When the tide was in, they surveyed the ARNOLD's skeleton with a magnetometer from a rowboat, with readings indicating many metal objects hidden below her deck. Reiss concluded that the wreck is "a late 18th century merchant ship, of about 200-ton burden, and certainly could have been used during the Revolutionary War as a privateer." In December Charlie Sanderson presented his arch- aeological plan for excavation of the GENERAL ARNOLD to the Board in Boston. "In 1986," he stated, "we hope to remove her deck and see what's in her hold, and if her cargo is still there, which we assume it is, it will provide us with a great window of knowledge into the 18th century... After all artifacts are recovered," he concluded, "we hope to raise the hull of the ARNOLD in one piece, as they did the VASSAR in Sweden," said Sanderson, "and display her at a museum in the Plymouth area".

Charlie Sanderson III and I walked out of the Board meeting together and onto Boston's busy Washington Street. Shoppers were pushing and grumbling under their frozen breath, carolers were singing, and Santa with a yellowed beard was clanging his bell on the corner. "I'll buy you a holiday drink, if you promise not to pour it into your shoes," Charlie smiled wryly. We headed for the "Last Hurrah" to drink a toast to Captain Jim Magee. It was Christmas, and it was snowing hard.

(top) Unidentified brig, like the ARNOLD, founders in the shallows. (lower left) At the mass-grave site of ARNOLD crew in Plymouth are, (from left to right) Al Janard, metal detecting expert, author Bob Cahill, Charles Sanderson III, who found the ARNOLD wreck, 13 year old Pat Hayes, diver Jay Barrett, and Arthur Chalifour. Photo by John Hayes. (lower right) nautical archaeologists inspect wreck of ARNOLD off Plymouth at dead-low tide. Photo by Charles Sanderson IV.

IV
LADIES OF THE LAKE

Only a few weeks after the Battle of Lexington and Concord, some 200 Vermont Green Mountain Boys had gathered at the banks of Lake Champlain to attack British held Fort Ticonderoga when Benedict Arnold arrived with the authority from the Commonwealth of Massachusetts to take command of the Vermont troops. Democracy prevailed; the "Boys" voted Arnold out and decided that Vermont's Ethan Allen would command them into battle, although they did allow Arnold to accompany them across the lake to the fort. Striking at dawn, May 10, 1775, the Green Mountain Boys literally caught the British garrison with its pants down and took the fort without firing a shot. Capturing British food supplies, ammunition, many swivel guns, a mortar and over 100 cannons, Ethan Allen became the hero of the day. To appease the ruffled feathers of Benedict Arnold, the Continental Congress placed him in command of the Lake Champlain navy.

At the southern end of the 118 mile long lake, the Americans built warships at Skenesboro, now Whitehall, New York; and at the northern end, at St. John's Quebec, the British developed a navy yard to build ships of war. By early October, 1776, Arnold's homemade fleet of 16 flat-bottomed gondolas, galleys and gunboats, manned by rag-tag crews of landlubbing militiamen, sailed out of Whitehall. From the north came a British flotilla, twice the size of Arnold's. When Arnold met the British near Isle la Motte, he realized it was hopeless to fight them, so he turned his boats around and headed back to home port. But on October 11th, near Crown Point, the British closed in and overtook him. There was no escape for the American flotilla, and within three days 12 vessels of Arnold's freshwater navy were sitting on the bottom of the lake.

Many of the American crewmen managed to escape by grounding their vessels, then intentionally sinking them along the Vermont shore at Otter Creek, now known as Arnold Bay in Panton. According to Arnold's battle report, "two gondolas sunk at Schuyler's Island, one sunk at Valcour Island, four scuttled on the Vermont shore and one escaped." The gondola that Arnold said had escaped was the JERSEY, but the British battle report lists the JERSEY as having been captured by them. Of the four vessels which avoided the wrath of the British and made it back to Whitehall the schooner REVENGE and gunboats GATES, ENTERPRISE, and NEW YORK were later scuttled at Whitehall to prevent them from being captured by the advancing British. It was a complete and crushing defeat for General Benedict Arnold, which surely helped his decision to eventually join what he considered an unbeatable enemy.

Arnold's flagship, the galley ROYAL SAVAGE, was found in 1932 in 15 feet of water only 200 feet off Valcour Island, by helmet diver and noted salvage engineer, Colonel Lorenzo Hagglund of New York. Initially, he collected many artifacts near the wreck and two years later returned to Vermont to salvage the ROYAL SAVAGE, or what was left of her. He brought up 40 feet of her hull, planking, ribs, keel, and over 100 artifacts, such as grapeshot, cannon balls, muskets, knives, cooking and eating utensils and nautical fittings. These articles are presently being stored in a Long Island barn by the colonel's son.

In 1935 Colonel Hagglund returned to Valcour Island and, using a dragging device from a surface yacht, he snagged the gondola PHILADELPHIA in 60 feet of water in the Valcour Bay Channel. When he dove down to take a look at his find, he saw the old gondola sitting in the bottom mud, her mast still upright after 159 years, her cannons in place — all in near-perfect condition, looking much like she did on the day she sank. He cradled her with ropes and winched her in one piece to the surface. Inside her the salvagers found tools, anchors, buttons, china dishes and cups, pewter spoons and even part of her canvas sail. These make up the most important collection of Revolutionary War artifacts ever found; and the ship herself is the oldest man-of-war ever recovered intact in United States waters. The PHILADELPHIA is now on permanent display at the Smithsonian Institution, Washington, D.C.

In 1967 Dr. Phillip Lundeberg, Curator of Naval History at the Smithsonian, with the help of the National Geographic Society, spent two weeks searching for the lost gondolas off Schuyler Island. Using Edgerton's side-scan sonar and a team of divers and archaeologists, Lundeberg uncovered only a few wooden fittings and some cannon balls; but the sunken vessels were not located. Others have searched since, but have also come up empty-handed.

Although the Colonials managed to salvage cannons and muskets from the five American and three British wrecks in Arnold Bay, soon after the battle, parts of the wrecks protruded above shallow water at low tide, well into the 19th century. Relic hunters began stripping these wrecks in the 1870's and continued to do so until the Vermont Historic Preservation Act was passed by the state legislature in 1975. This Act gives the state title to all underwater wrecks and artifacts, and mandates through the Division for Historic Preservation that all wreck hunters obtain a permit for underwater exploration and recovery of any historic items. Prior to the passage of the act, however, the galley CONGRESS was raised in one piece from the Bay and then cut up into pieces for souvenir hunters. Also, two other American gunboats were salvaged from the shallows in the early 1900s, and they, too, were carted away piece by piece by locals and tourists wanting keepsakes of the Revolutionary War. In 1952 a gondola was recovered intact from Arnold Bay, as well as hundreds of artifacts such as tools, eating utensils, muskets and munitions, all of which are presently being stored in a barn at Willsboro, Vermont for hopeful future display in a museum.

The Champlain Maritime Society, a non-profit volunteer organization of Burlington, Vermont is presently hunting for a unique British vessel that participated in Arnold's defeat at the Battle of Valcour, but was lost a year later, November 8, 1777, when she hit a rock west of Alburg, Vermont. She was the 90-foot THUNDERER, a floating platform carrying munitions and hospital supplies. Before she sank, blown off course by heavy winds on her way to Canada, another British vessel rescued her crew and some supplies. This one-of-a-kind Revolutionary War platform-vessel awaits discovery in the depths of Lake Champlain.

The Champlain Maritime Society conducted a successful side-scan sonar survey and underwater hunt at Whitehall in 1982-83. They found twenty sunken vessels in the narrows between Lock 12 of the Champlain Canal and Benson's Landing. A few of the wrecks were 19th century commercial barges, but many were remnants of America's War of 1812 lake fleet which were left to rot at Whitehall after the War, including the 20-gun ship EAGLE and the captured British gunboat LINNET. The team of divers and archaeologists also located one of Arnold's sunken gunboats. Scuba diver Jim Kennard reported that although most of the wrecks were twenty or more feet underwater, "some were as close as two feet from the surface."

Jim Kennard and his side-scan sonar also helped to locate the 146-foot sidewheel steamboat PHOENIX, the second steamboat to ply the waters of Lake Champlain in 1815. She caught fire off Colchester Point four years later, drifted onto the rocks and sank, six of the 52 people aboard her going down with the ship. Scuba divers have periodically visited her charred remains at 110 feet within the last six years, bringing up many early 19th century artifacts. Slowly but surely, the PHOENIX is rising from her ashes.

Scuba divers Scott McDonald and Dean Russell found the remarkably preserved 88-foot wreck of the schooner rigged merchant vessel GENERAL BUTLER in August 1980. Carrying a cargo of marble from the famous Isle la Motte quarries, she hit the Burlington break-water in a violent gale on December 17, 1876. Her captain, four crew members and two women passengers managed to leap to safety onto the breakwater before the ship went under. The divers found her masts still standing upright and discovered that they were stepped above the deck, designed to fold down when the ship passed under canal bridges. Entering the wreck, they found many cabins still intact, including the sleeping quarters, where they recovered a small whiskey flask and a large chamber pot. Other artifacts brought to the surface were ironstone dishes, glasses, crockery, eating utensils, a large iron cooking pot, a jug, wine bottles, more liquor flasks and part of a woolen shirt — all remark-ably preserved in the fresh cold water, where wood-eating worms and electrolysis do not destroy artifacts as they do in salt water. All items recovered from the GENERAL BUTLER are being preserved by the state of Vermont for future public exhibit.

Another tiller-steered, mast-stepped marble vessel was discovered a year earlier off Burlington in 50 feet of water by Canadian nautical archaeologist Marc Theoret, with the help of Dr. Harold Edgerton and his side-scan sonar. Theoret was searching for three sunken War of 1812 ships when he stumbled upon this unknown 79-foot long wreck. Remarkably preserved, her hold was still filled with marble from Isle la Motte, and her cabins, hatches, doors and deck all in place. Artifacts much like those found on the GENERAL BUTLER are being collected and preserved by Vermont's Division for Historic Preservation.

Meanwhile, Old Doc Edgerton with his side-scan sonar is looking for the steamboat AUNT SALLY at Lake Morey, Vermont. The lake is named after inventor Samuel Morey, who in 1797 built a steamboat which he tried to sell to Robert Fulton. Fulton wouldn't buy, but Morey claimed for the rest of his life that Fulton stole his idea. In 1820 Morey's steamboat AUNT SALLY sank into what was then known as Fairlee Pond. Edgerton, who has thus far charted the entire lake with his sonar, is bent on finding AUNT SALLY.

Recently, diver Jim Kennard, Scott Hill and Joseph "Zar" Zarzynski, with the aid of a side-scan sonar, located the remains of the 258-foot paddlewheel steamer CHAMPLAIN in 40 feet of water off Westport, New York. She was heading out of Westport for Burlington, Vermont when she struck a rock called "the mountain" at Steam Mill Point on July 15, 1875. "The wreck was caused," explained second pilot Eli Rockwell, "by the fact that Pilot John Eldredge, a sufferer from the gout, had been quietly taking drugs, and he fell asleep at the wheel." Rockwell goes on to report, "the steamer's bow was out of water and she had broken her back. The after end was under water up to the salon deck. The galley and dining room were all under water, but the Captain said if we could get into the upper end of the dining room we could get some food. So, we cut a hole through the bulkhead to put a small waiter through, but he came back aflying and said there was a dead man in there. We cut the hole larger and I went in. There was a man lying on the berth. The side of the ship was stove in within two feet of his head. About four feet of water was in the room and his shoes were floating in it. I shook him and he woke up... He was a law student who had just passed his bar exam. He had been celebrating, and had slept through all the wreck."

Kennard, Hill and Zarzynski plan to explore the wreck further for artifacts, and surely — as seems to be the case in most Lake Champlain wrecks — they will find rum jugs, wine bottles and whiskey flasks. In fact, Ethan Allen and his Green Mountain Boys were heavy drinkers, carrying rum and whiskey into battle with them. Benedict Arnold, on the other hand, preferred tea, which could have been an added cause to his downfall. If it weren't for Arnold, however, there wouldn't be so many interesting wrecks and artifacts to search for in Lake Champlain.

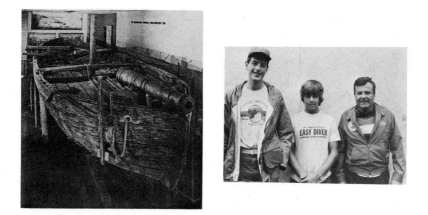

The preserved Lake Champlain gunboat PHILADELPHIA, now on display at Smithsonian Institution, Washington. Scuba divers Joe Zarzynski, Jack Sullivan and son, Lake Champlain wreck hunters.

V
NEW HAMPSHIRE'S ISLES OF SHOALS

The improbable names of Appledore, Smuttynose, Lunging, Cedar, White, Star, and Duck make up the small windswept islands known as the Isles of Shoals, located ten miles off the coast of Portsmouth, New Hampshire.

I have visited these islands many times within the last 30 years, each time searching for treasure. Most of my activities there have been underwater, combing the surrounding turbulent sea for the remains of old Spanish ships. The sea bottom around the Isles is covered with thick ribbony kelp, flowing from rock gullies that drop off from 20 feet to depths of 200 feet or more. Although I have never found even a splinter of wood from the treasure laden galleons, there is no doubt that they are there, possibly in deeper water than where I was hunting, or perfectly concealed within the kelp beds. I have also concluded that all the time I spent searching the sea bottom might have been better spent looking for treasure on the islands with a metal detector, for the bulk of treasure found at the Isles thus far has been dug up from the earth. Although the islands are mostly rocky and have little sand or dirt covering them, the silver bars and coins that have been recovered were either buried by pirates, or swept up from the depths during storms and deposited onto the islands.

The Isles of Shoals of today are as explorer Captain John Smith found them in 1614, "heaped together with none others near them, and many a barren rock, the most overgrown with shrubs, but without either grass or wood." Smith did mention in his diary that he saw, "three short shrubby old cedars," and one man tried to start an apple orchard there in the 19th century, but today there are just a few shrubby trees on the Isles.

Many pirate ships visited the Isles in the late 17th and throughout the 18th centuries. Old records seem to indicate that the few fishermen who lived on the larger islands fed and indulged these "gentlemen-of-fortune" in every way. Edward Teach, better known as Blackbeard, was a periodic visitor to the Isles, as were Ned Low, William Kidd, and Black Sam Bellamy of WHYDAH fame. Phillip Babb — one of Captain Kidd's first mates — settled on Appledore Island soon after Kidd was sent off to England in chains to be hanged. According to New Hampshire historian Oscar Laighton: "When Babb first came to Appledore there was a large excavation at the head of the cove," near Babb's house. "Babb made a big effort to dig up something. The pit he made was thirty feet across and ten feet deep, as I remember it, but the place was filled up level in the great storm of 1851." Early in this century the Coast Guard built a boathouse over the spot of Babb's treasure pit.

In 1720, Blackbeard was almost captured at the Isles by a British warship. He and his crew had stopped off at Star Island to replenish their food supply, but were forced into a hasty retreat when the British ship came into view. They departed in such a hurry that Blackbeard left his girlfriend Martha Herring behind. She, according to legend, remained at the Isles for 15 years, awaiting the return of her ferocious lover. He never showed up, and she died of heartbreak at White Island in 1735.

In 1950, *Life Magazine* published a story that pirate Captain Quelch buried a treasure of $100,000 in gold and silver at the Isles, but the magazine article did not divulge the source of this information. It is well documented, however, that Quelch in his brig CHARLES, did frequent the Isles during the late 17th century. Although most of his pirate crew escaped at Marblehead, Massachusetts, he and a few of the crew were captured after a brief visit to the Isles and hanged at Boston in 1704.

Only one person lived on Smuttynose Island in 1813, and that was Sam Haley. On stormy nights he would keep lanterns burning in the windows of his home that faced the open sea. The lights, he hoped, would help vessels avoid the treacherous shoals. On the morning of January 15, 1813, Sam found the frozen body of a ship-wrecked sailor lying in the drifting snow in front of his house. The Spanish sailor had dropped dead from exposure only a few feet from his front door. In the night, a Spanish galleon heading for Spain from Portsmouth hit Cedar Island Ledge, only a few hundred yards from Sam Haley's home. Sam had slept soundly through the stormy night, not hearing the ripping of timbers as the galleon was crushed by the rocks, nor the screams of the frightened Spaniards. Only 14 bodies washed ashore: there were no survivors. Grave markers covered with weed and a crude rock monument still stand in memory of these unknown Spaniards on the windswept island of Smuttynose. There had been 28 crewmen aboard the 400 ton galleon CONCEPTION, under the command of don Juan Coxava, when she wrecked that night, but even well into this century there was confusion as to whether it was the Spanish vessel SAGUNTO or the Cadiz galleon CONCEPTION that wrecked off Sam Haley's house. Both had traveled up the coast from the West Indies to Portsmouth, New Hampshire to add dried fish to their cargoes, and both had slipped out of port heading for Spain on the night of January 14th. The SAGUNTO apparently made it by the Isles and put into Newport, Rhode Island, rather than sailing out the storm, so says historian Samuel Adams Drake, but the CONCEPTION disappeared, and it is thought to be this vessel that had crashed into Cedar Island Ledge. For ten days after the storm, much wreckage drifted ashore at the Eastern point of Smuttynose and into the wash between Smuttynose and Appledore Islands: raisins, oranges, wood, cloth, clothes, and a few silver pieces-of-eight.

It was three years after the shipwreck, in 1816, that Sam Haley, Jr. — old Sam's son — got permission from the Massachusetts legislature to build, "a sufficient sea-wall around the dock where the said Haley now lives." While building this seawall that connects Smuttynose with Cedar Island, providing a harbor between these islands, Sam Haley Jr. found four silver bars. They were hidden under rocks on the island's south beach. He sold them for $4,000. It was this find that started people thinking that the CONCEPTION carried a cargo more fruitful than oranges and raisins. The bars could have been hidden by pirates, but most thought they had washed onto the beach from the 1813 wreck.

In 1901, while she was vacationing on Star Island, Mrs. James Allen found three Spanish gold doubloons dated 1600, which had probably been washed up in a storm from a Spanish galleon that wrecked near the northside cliffs facing Halfway Rocks in 1685. A church was built on the southwest side of Star Island from the wood that washed ashore from this wreck, and part of this church is still standing today.

From 1865 through 1869, blackened Spanish coins of silver washed ashore on the southside beach at Appledore Island, facing Smuttynose, and until a few of the coins were cleaned, it was thought that they came from the CONCEPTION; but they all dated in the 1700s, over 100 years before the CONCEPTION sank. Possibly another unknown Spanish vessel carrying treasure from South America or the West Indies, wrecked at the Isles near Appledore Island in the 18th century. Codfish and other local fish, salted and dried by the fishermen of Portsmouth and the Isles, was a great favorite of the Spanish. In fact, many Spanish ships laden with treasures from the tropical New World would stop off at New Hampshire before traveling on to the Old World with their gold, silver, and dried fish to please the King of Spain.

In 1870, a clay pot with 60 Spanish silver coins in it was dug up on Star Island. This, without a doubt, was the hidden catch of some old pirate. There were probably many other pots filled with treasure dug up at the Isles that nobody but the finder knows about.

There is only one snug harbor at the Isles, called Gosport, surrounded by Smuttynose, Cedar, and Star Islands. Here, scuba divers from Portsmouth recently found a few fistfuls of coins, some brass and copper, and a few silver. Because one or two were dated in the early 1800s, it is thought that they washed into the harbor from Cedar Island Ledge before Sam Haley built his seawall. However, since many of these coins are British, they are probably from still another unknown or forgotten shipwreck off the Isles.

There are a few houses, mostly summer cottages, on the bigger islands at the Isles of Shoals, a rickety old wooden hotel on Star Island, and a lighthouse on White Island. Otherwise the Isles are deserted — except, of course, for the ghosts of Phillip Babb and Martha Herring, who respectively guard the buried treasures of Captain Kidd and Blackbeard. There is, without doubt, much of value to be recovered from these islands, on land and in the surrounding sea. If New England, like the West Indies and Nova Scotia, would like to claim fame to its own genuine treasure islands, they are New Hampshire's Isles of Shoals.

APPLEDORE ISLAND

DIVING OPERATIONS
◉ 1954

GOSPORT HARBOR   SILVER BARS 1820   SMUTTYNOSE ISLE

CEDAR ISLAND
◉ WRECK RUSSIAN SHIP

LUNGING ISLAND

STAR ISLAND
WRECK SPANISH 1685

WRECK ◉ SPANISH GALLEON 1813

WHITE ISLAND

ISLES OF SHOALS

Map locates four sunken British warships off Rhode Island. Model is of the CERBERUS, one of the four, scuttled in Narragansett Bay.

Al Davis and Dr. Foster Middleton (left) examine artifacts from the CERBERUS. Photos courtesy the University of Rhode Island.

VI
RHODE ISLAND'S REVOLUTIONARY WAR WRECKS

The charred and waterlogged hulls of four British warships rest peacefully, undisturbed for over 205 years, in the shallows near Newport, Rhode Island. They are the LARK, CERBERUS, OR-PHEUS, and JUNO. They were once proud ships-of-the-line, harassing New England's maritime efforts during the early years of America's War for Independence. Today they are registered National Historical Sites, yet they are under some 20 feet of water and six feet of bottom silt where no one can see them, and few know their exact locations.

The British had fortified Rhode Island at Newport and expected an attack by the Americans. They were prepared to deal with George Washington's little, often mutinous Navy, but they were not ready to deal with what greeted them on the morning of July 28, 1778. Over the horizon sailing for Newport were 16 large and well armed vessels, eager and able to purge the British from their Rhode Island fort. Terror swept through Newport — it wasn't the rag tag American rebels who were coming to do battle, but Count D'Estaing, commanding twelve French ships-of-the-line and four French frigates, an awesome fleet that would easily destroy or capture the seven British ships anchored up river.

On July 29, one day after the French fleet appeared off Newport, the British were forced, for fear of capture, to destroy two fine galleys and a sloop in the Sakonnet River. A few days later several French warships rounded the northern tip of Conanicut Island in Narragansett Bay and sailed rapidly up the bay towards the four anchored British frigates — CERBERUS, LARK, ORPHEUS and JUNO. British lookouts spotted them coming and ordered all ships to weigh anchor and get under sail in an attempt to reach the protective shore batteries at Newport some six miles to the south. Luck was not with the British this day, as both tide and wind were against them. Under strict admiralty orders not to let their vessels fall into enemy hands, the British com-manders took the only alternative open to them — they turned their oak hulled vessels eastward and ran them against the rocky coastline of Aquidneck Island. As the French continued their pursuit, the British captains off-loaded their crews, cut the masts of their frigates, then set them aflame. All four vessels sank within a few miles of each other. The Battle of Rhode Island continued on for eight days, the French persisting in their harassment of the Newport fortification until August 9, when they then sailed out of Rhode Island Sound to engage British Lord Howe's reinforced fleet from New York.

The British never attempted to salvage their four frigates from the shallow water, and after the Revolutionary War, the Americans either weren't interested or couldn't find the sunken men-o-war. It wasn't until 1970 that one man, Al Davis, Jr. of Kingstown, Rhode Island, realized the value of these sunken ships and went looking for them. He began his search in the local library, researching all available literature on the battle. There he found an old chart giving the approximate locations of the forgotten vessels. Wearing scuba, Al Davis began probing the murky waters of Narragansett Bay for 18th century British artifacts. Unable to afford modern underwater detection gear, Al played a hunch that some small portion of each wreck would still be protruding from the Bay's muddy bottom. Although they are separated by almost three miles, the LARK and CERBERUS were selected as his two primary targets. The bottom, where the chart located them, is harder, and there is less sediment accumulation there than where the ORPHEUS and JUNO went down.

Three years of diving almost every weekend, except in winter, yeilded only a few small artifacts — a copper barrel hoop, a few spikes and two cannon balls; but they were enough to encourage Davis to continue his search into the fourth year. At the time, he was also completing studies for a master's degree in Ocean Engineering at the University of Rhode Island, and he asked faculty members and fellow students at the university to help in his quest. Al's father also became interested and took a trip to England to scour dusty old logs, journals and diarys in British museums and libraries for further information to pinpoint the exact locations of the wrecks. Al Davis, Sr. obtained a reproduction of an accurate wreck site map at the British Museum and — even more important — a transcript of the original log of the H.M.S. CERBERUS from the Greenwich Maritime Museum. The transcript was the key to finding the wreck site of the CERBERUS, for it mentioned that, "the crew stood on the brow of a hill and watched their vessel burn and explode. . ."

Al Davis, Jr. and his buddy diver Russ Walker, walked the coastline looking for the appropriate "brow" where the British sailors watched their ship go down until they found it, almost three-quarters of a mile south of the position indicated on the first chart at the local library. Al and Russ donned their scuba gear immediately and plunged in. On the second day of combing the bottom, they found the ballast heap of the CERBERUS in 20 feet of water only a few yards offshore, surrounded by heavy oak planking. Then they came upon a swivel gun. In deeper water, cannons littered the bottom — two 800 pound cannons and one enormous 2,700 pounder with a family of lobsters living in the muzzle. At the base of this black cast iron gun was the design of the British broad arrow scrolled crown seal of King George, weight markings and the English foundry identification.

Realizing both the financial and legal problems that a find of this magnitude entails, Davis decided not to begin excavation of the CERBERUS right away. Keeping her location secret, he went on to search for the LARK. With the help of the map his father had obtained in London, he located the rotting timbers and ballast pile of the LARK within two weeks of finding the CERBERUS. She also had heavy cannons strewn for 50 yards around her shallow water grave site.

The University of Rhode Island, under the direction of Dr. Foster Middleton, took on the responsibility of excavating the wrecks, receiving initial funding from the National Science Foundation. This allowed Al Davis and Brad Alton, Assistant Director of the project, to obtain proper permits, endorsements and equipment necessary for an extensive salvage project and to purchase the proper preservatives for all artifacts they hoped to bring up. When Al and Brad were not busy with paper work and equipment design for the archaeological dig, they were underwater at one of the two wreck sites. Initial stages of the project consisted primarily of acoustical probing of the sites with underwater instruments such as sparkers, pingers and side-scan sonar. Then the University decided to work initially on the salvage of articles from the CERBERUS because she was in shallower water and nearer to shore than the LARK.

The first items raised to the surface were three large cannons, one of which had rusted before it could be properly coated with preservatives. A pewter English teapot covered with sea growth was found under layers of bottom silt. Then some wine and rum bottles were uncovered by the divers as they dug into the rock ballast. Hand grenades with the fabric wicking still intact were brought up, along with lignum-vitae pully sheaves with bronze bushings, leather shoes, sealskin boots, a few worn copper coins, ballast bars, cannon balls with the British broad arrow embossed in them and a musket plate with the date 1746 on it.

After spending the summer probing into the wreck of the CERBERUS, with an occasional dive on the LARK, Al Davis decided to spend the cold months trying to find the 708-ton ORPHEUS, the largest of the British vessels scuttled in Narragansett Bay. Like his dad, he decided that the best place to research was England; so he hopped a plane to London. During a thorough search of old documents at the

London Public Records Office, he came upon the court martial test-imonies of all the British captains who lost their vessels in Rhode Island waters. Among the many interesting facts presented in these records, Al was excited by the statement of the captain of the ORPHEUS, which read: "Time did not allow the removal of the crew's hammocks or personal belongings, prior to the ship's destruction. . ." This meant that the wreck of the ORPHEUS, and probably most of the other sunken vessels as well, contained all the personal effects of the officers and crew members. Al couldn't wait for Spring to begin his underwater search. He flew back to New England and was in the cold water the next day. After only two hours of searching, he found the ORPHEUS.

Like the other two wrecks, the ORPHEUS was surrounded by cannons weighing almost 3,000 pounds. Her oak timbers, unlike those of the other two, were well preserved, though covered with some seven feet of bottom sediment. Al was ready for the long tedious task of getting permission from the state and federal governments to properly excavate the wreck. To his great disappointment, however, he discovered that all available money for such projects had run out, and there was no further funding available for salvage of artifacts on any of the wrecks he had found.

Al Davis is now in Texas working in ocean engineering. Every once in a while the Rhode Island National Guard flies over the wreck sites of the CERBERUS and LARK to discourage any scuba-diving pirates, and periodically the State's Fish and Game Department boat patrols the sites in the summer time. Otherwise, the CERBERUS, LARK, ORPHEUS and JUNO, plus the three British ships in the Sakonnet River remain underwater and undisturbed. Not the sea, but government red tape, lack of adequate funds and archaeological dis-interest has conquered these wrecks and their historical treasures.

"It is frustrating knowing so many historically valuable artifacts and personal belongings of British seamen are buried under the sediment, and it's a shame that the project that could make them available for public enjoyment and education has collapsed," says Al Davis. Hope-fully, some day Al's dream will come true.

UP AND DOWN THE COAST
From Maine to Connecticut

When Miles Standish entered Boston Harbor in his small sailboat on September 29, 1621, he realized that he wasn't the first white man to visit these shores. Explorer John Smith had been here seven years before, and Smith mentions in his journal that "a French ship has shortly before been here and remained six weeks, trading with the natives." Another French trading vessel ventured into Boston Harbor in 1616, anchored off Peddocks Island, and the crew awaited the Indians who paddled out to greet them in fur-filled canoes. Monsieur Finch, commander of the ship, had a horrible surprise in store when, as Cotton Mather tells us, "those bloody savages, with knives concealed under flaps, immediately butchered all his men and set the ship on fire." Governor Winthrop in his *History of New England (1630 to 1649)* writes that, "a Mr. Ludlow, in digging the foundation of his house at Dorchester Bay, found two pieces of French money; one was coined in 1596. They were in several places and above a foot within the firm ground." These coins probably came from the French ship destroyed by Indians off Peddocks Island in Dorchester Bay, part of Boston Harbor.

In 1919 at Lovell's Island, also in Boston Harbor, lighthouse keeper Charles Jennings dug out of his vegetable garden 14 French silver and gold coins, all dating between 1660 and 1775. These, without doubt, came from the man-o-war MAGNIFIQUE that sailed into Boston Harbor with the French fleet on August 15, 1782. The MAGNIFIQUE, carrying 74 cannons, was a shipwright's masterpiece, a gift to revolutionary America from France. When she reached the Boston dock, John Paul Jones, who was waiting on shore, would take command of her. Boston pilot, David Darling, was bringing her in, for the French didn't know the ins and outs of the harbor. Darling put her on the rocks and the magnificent frigate sank within an hour, leaving Jones without a ship and Darling without a job. Although most of her cannons were recovered, all attempts to salvage the vessel failed. The currents and rips around Lovell's Island were then, and are now, swift and treacherous; they soon buried the MAGNIFIQUE under mud and silt. Within 100 years, the build-up of debris over the wreck created a peninsula — the perfect place for a lighthouse. Thus, keeper Jennings found coins from the wreck buried in his garden. Deep in the hold of the buried MAGNIFIQUE was a vault containing $300,000 in gold and silver coins, another gift from the French to the Americans that never made port. But the lighthouse keeper didn't get it all. There should be a fortune buried under the lighthouse.

Diver Duggie Russell was hired a few years ago, to dive outside Salem Harbor in search of a water-logged trunk which had been snagged accidentally by lobsterman Nick Vaccaro while pulling traps on the seaward side of Misery Island off Manchester. Nick managed to haul the trunk to the surface; but it was too heavy to lift aboard his boat, and he lost it. He described the trunk as typical of the 18th century, "used by the elite when taking long sea voyages." Duggie spent over two hours searching the kelpy bottom off Misery but could not locate the trunk, probably from the brig JOHN that struck the eastern point of Misery Island at night in a snowstorm on January 11, 1796. The 87-ton brig immediately went to pieces. The Salem newspaper next day reported, "Crew all saved, as well as Captain Edward Allen, a passenger, 62 days out from London." The trunk hauled in and then lost overboard by Nick Vaccaro probably belonged to Captain Allen.

On that same stormy evening two similar trunks were driven ashore at Little Good Harbor Beach, Gloucester — one containing clothes and letters, the other 119 gold guineas. These trunks came not from the brig JOHN, but from the ship INDUSTRY that disappeared beneath the waves off Salt Island — none of her 14-man crew survived. In the very same storm, the great ship MARGARET, sailing home to Boston from Amsterdam with a valuable cargo of gin and china, crashed into the Gooseberries, on outcropping of rocks near Bakers Island. Her captain, John Mackay, like the skippers of the JOHN and the INDUSTRY, was blinded by the blizzard and mistook the entrance to Salem Harbor as the entrance to Boston Harbor. He and three of his crewmen drowned as the ship broke to pieces. The others managed to make Bakers and were rescued hours later by Marblehead fishermen. No one searched for the wreck until the summer of 1983, when scuba divers Jay Barrett and Dennis Loger spent almost every Saturday of the summer searching in and around the reefs and rock islands of the Gooseberries. They searched in 1984 and 1985 but have yet to find a sliver of china, nor a drop of Holland gin.

"Only two leagues from Plum Island," reveals a Revolutionary War document at the Newburyport Library, "near the mouth of the Merrimack River," is the marvelous sunken prize NEPTUNE. Barrett and Loger are searching for this 1778 privateer too. Rigged for battle, she sailed out of Newburyport on her maiden voyage. With the "hurrahs" of the townfolks still echoing in the ears of the crew, the NEPTUNE hit a freak wave and nosed under, never to return to the surface again. All of her crew but one was able to swim ashore. When the NEPTUNE is found, she'll be an archaeologist's dream come true.

At Plum Island, All Locke and Sheldon Lane, using metal detectors recently came upon an old timber near the Bar Head breakwater. It was obviously the remains of an old ship washed ashore in a recent storm. Locke passed his metal detector over the rotting wood and surprisingly got a reading. He dug his knife into the wood expecting to find an old nail or spike but instead dug out a partially worn bronze coin, about the size of an American half dollar. The coin had a strange foreign inscription on it, so he brought it to James Whittall of Rowley, an archaeologist and director of the Early Sites Research Society. Whittall recognized it as a "Roman Setterii" minted in the third century A.D. The embossed portrait on one side of the coin was of Emperor Gordian III, who ruled the Roman Empire from 238 to 244. Locke and Lane returned to Bar Head, Plum Island, but the sea had carried away their mysterious ancient timber. Peter Pratt, a coin dealer in Georgetown, hearing of the find, contacted Jim Whittall and revealed that he too had found a Roman Setterii on Plum Island in 1974 at the southern tip of the island, only 200 yards from where Al Locke had dug his coin out of the rotting ship's timber. Another Roman coin was found there in September, 1985. Four other Roman coins, dating from 337 to 383 A.D. were found in a clump at Dane Street Beach in Beverly in 1977.

In 1971 at Castine Bay, Maine a unique discovery was made by scuba diver Norwood Bakeman. While combing the muddy bottom for old bottles, Bakeman stumbled upon two large ceramic storage jars. He brought them up and delivered them to the University of Maine, where they were displayed for a few years. But nobody seemed to know what they were, how old they were or how valuable they were, so interest in them waned. Six years later, however, Jim Whittall heard about Bakeman's jars and drove up to Maine to inspect them. He recognized them immediately as anforeta. "In all probability very ancient," says Whittall, "and they may have come from the coastal area of the Southern Iberian Penninsula." Whittall and Harvard professor Dr. Barry Fell believe it quite within reason that ancient Phoenician traders or Iberian-Celtic mercahnts had come to North America to barter with the Indians centuries before Columbus. Marks around the edges of the Castine anforeta jars show wear from constant chafing, probably caused by the rolling of the vessel at sea while the jars were secured by lines to the deck or in the hold. Doctor Fell was recently called out to Monhegan Island off the coast of Maine by local anthropologists to decipher an inscription on a large sea-side boulder uncovered there. The strange writing chiseled into the rock, Dr. Fell concluded, is ancient Celtic and reads "Cargo Platforms for ships from Phoenicia."

Two other anforeta jars like the ones Bakeman found were uncovered in areas that at one time were underwater. One dug up while workmen were building the underground garage at Boston Common is now on display at Boston University; the other was pulled out of the mud on the Boston shore when the Southeast Expressway was being constructed. Could it be that the Boston Celtics were here centuries before the Pilgrims, Puritans and our Boston patriots?

Many historians believe that a wreck recently uncovered off Marshfield, Massachusetts by scuba diver Jim Baldi could be the find of the century. Baldi claimed his find through the Massachusetts Board of Underwater Archaeology but has yet to begin excavating the wreck. He thinks it is a French merchant ship wrecked in a storm around 1616. Prior to his finding of old timbers sticking out of the bottom sand at a depth of 40 feet, other interesting items had been hauled up in the same area by fishermen. Part of a conquistador's helmet was netted from the depths off Marshfield in the early 1900s, and a large iron claw, used as a lantern on ancient vessels, was dragged up by fishermen in 1944. By accident in 1952 a Brant Rock lobsterman pulled up a large encrusted bronze shield. It was covered with thick layers of sea growth, but once the crust was removed, the face of the shield revealed carvings of charging horses and dueling warriors. One archaeologist who saw the shield believes it may be Phoenician, Roman or possibly Ancient Celtic. Baldi has uncovered pewter spoons, cannon balls, doughnut shaped pullies and other artifacts from the bottom sand around his wreck, but until the wreck itself is uncovered, the vessel's date, name and origin remain a mystery. There is no doubt, however, that she predates the MAYFLOWER, and may add a new chapter to American history books.

Approximately 65 miles straight out to sea from the WHYDAH, off Wellfleet, is an extremely controversial sunken ship, supposedly containing six tons of gold. Four diving teams are competing for her treasure, and members of two of these teams claim to have visited the wreck in June and August 1983. She was the luxurious British White Star liner REPUBLIC that sank into 235 feet of water after colliding with the steamer FLORIDA on January 24, 1909. The REPUBLIC was out of New York heading for Greece with 600 passengers aboard and $3,000,000 in double-eagle ten dollar gold pieces stashed in the liner's vaults. The 8,000-ton FLORIDA was coming from Italy, cruising slowly through a thick fog, when she sliced into the 585-foot REPUBLIC. Thanks to John Binns, the liner's radio operator, using the newly installed Marconi wireless, many rescue ships arrived shortly on the scene, and only four people lost their lives. This was the first time Marconi's new invention was used for sea rescue.

There was an attempt to tow the REPUBLIC into Nantucket, but 39 hours after the collision, while under tow, she sank. At the time of her sinking, however, the ship's paymaster would not confirm that the gold was aboard. Divers Stuart Brooks of Florida, Russ Langella of New Jersey, Martin Barerle of Massachusetts and Greg Horton and Chip Geisel of Connecticut have all searched diligently over the years for the REPUBLIC, and all claim they have pinpointed her location. Two of the above reported that they visited the wreck in 1985, but recovering the gold from that deep, muddy water, plagued by sharks and swift currents, is quite another task. What is surely prompting them on, is that the gold coins are worth about $120,000,000 today — if they are still there.

Some 45 miles south of Nantucket Island not far from the sunken REPUBLIC is another luxury liner, the "unsinkable" 690-foot AN-DREA DORIA. Resting at a depth of 240 feet, she has become for scuba divers what the Mattahorn is for mountain climbers; yet fewer than 30 men have visited her in her sunken tomb, most of them searching for treasure — priceless paintings, a purser's safe stuffed with money and jewelry. The smaller Banco di Roma safe, containing soaked and blackened $20 bills, was opened during a premiere television show in 1984, but yet to be recovered are silver relief plaques on the chapel walls, Chrysler's one-of-a-kind $100,000 idea car and many other items and artifacts worth a small fortune. New York diver Peter Gimble was the first to visit the DORIA less than 24 hours after she sank due to a collision with the Swedish liner STOCKHOLM on the evening of July 25, 1956. Gimble, with buddy diver Joe Fox, took underwater photographs for *Life Magazine*. Gimble, with California diver Jack McKenny, returned to dive the DORIA in 1981, and after five weeks of digging into the bowels of the liner, they located the purser's safe and the Banco di Roma safe. The first was too heavy to lift, but the latter safe they managed to winch to the surface. After spending almost two million dollars on the treasure hunting expedition, Gimble was disappointed that the smaller safe didn't reveal more, but he now plans to salvage the heavy purser's safe.

The only other treasure brought up from the DORIA was Italian Admiral Andrea Doria himself — a life-size bronze statue of him that was hacked off its pedestal on the promenade deck by scuba divers in

1964. The Admiral was hoisted to the surface, and, so I'm told, now graces the lawn-garden of a home in New Jersey.

Connecticut has its own Revolutionary War privateer DEFENCE off Stonington, like the DEFENCE recently found and excavated off Castine, Maine. The Connecticut DEFENCE was skippered by a tough old privateersman named Sam Smedley. While returning to home port in a storm after plundering six enemy vessels, Sam smashed his vessel into Bartlett's Reef. The DEFENCE, overloaded with British guns and silver, quickly sank to the bottom on March 10, 1779, taking Sam Smedley and the crew down with her. New York divers Ray Wagner and Howell Brose tried to find her but were unsuccessful. They did, however, find the rotted remains of another old ship off Long Shoal, Old Saybrook. Searching the old timbers of this unknown vessel at a depth of 80 feet, they found and brought to the surface two silver bars.

A team of New York divers recently discoverd another treasured shipwreck off Norwalk, Connecticut. In June 1982 a fisherman, trawling between Norwalk and Port Jefferson, Long Island, snagged a large anchor and hauled it aboard. He sold it for junk, but scuba diver Clive Cussler, author of the novel *Raise the Titanic*, traced the old anchor to the scrape pile. He bought it and identified it as the anchor from Cornelius Vanderbilt's famous paddle-wheel steamer LEXINGTON, known in pre-Civil War days as, "The White Lady." She caught fire steaming from New York to Stonington and disappeared in Long Island Sound on January 13, 1840. Only four of the 154 people aboard her lived to tell of her sinking. One survivor was David Crowley, who used one of the bales of cotton the LEXINGTON was carrying as a life-raft. Crowley drifted in the Sound for over 24 hours and almost froze to death until his cotton raft touched ashore at Long Island. Crowley reported that after the fire broke out, the captain tried to race the 200-foot steamer to the nearest shore in hopes of beaching her, and at the same time passengers tried to lower the lifeboats. The LEXINGTON was moving too fast to lower boats, the boats swamped, and all the passengers in them drowned. Shipping magnate Commodore Vanderbilt's "pride-of-the-fleet" never made it to the beach.

"She's one of the most unique and valuable ships ever lost at sea," announced Clive Cussler after tracking down the anchor, "and I'm going to find her." He began his diligent search in May of 1983 using a side-scan sonar and starting where the fisherman hauled up the anchor. Divers from Port Jefferson assisted him, but it wasn't until September 24, 1983 that the sonar revealed a large object sitting some 15 feet above the bottom mud at a depth of 60 feet, four miles off Stoney Brook. Cussler and his divers went down to investigate, and there was the LEXINGTON. She was broken into three pieces, charred from the fire and half buried in the mud, "but," says Cussler, "she's in remarkably good condition." The divers brought up pieces of charred yellow pine to positively identify her as the LEXINGTON. "It's the greatest underwater discovery of the century," said Cussler, and maybe he's right, for the wreck will surely reveal many wonderful artifacts, and her safe may contain the $105,000 in silver that was stashed in it when the ship left port. Cussler began excavating the wreck in 1985, and the Vanderbilt Museum in Centerport, Long Island will display the artifacts recovered.

The LEXINGTON, however, is only one of the thousands of valuable shipwrecks off the New England coast awaiting discovery and excavation. Clive Cussler is a good example of how patience, persistence and proper researching can turn fiction into fact.

The 656-foot ANDREA DORIA sinks off Nantucket in July, 1956. Divers Jack Clark and Don Rodocker visit the sunken DORIA in 1973. Photos courtesy the U.S. Coast Guard and Jack McKenney.

Bronze Shield, Marshfield, MA

Anforeta, Castine, Maine

Roman Coin, Plum Island, MA

Admiral Doria returns to Nantucket.

Photos courtesy of Malcolm Pearson, Edward Rowe Snow and Paul Tzimoulis.